the

**past explored**

Page 1. Eifl from Porth Dinllaen;
1. Standing stone, Llwyndyrys;
2. Pwllheli; 3. Sailing along the coast

# Llŷn
## the peninsula and its past explored

**Ioan Roberts**

Gwasg Carreg Gwalch

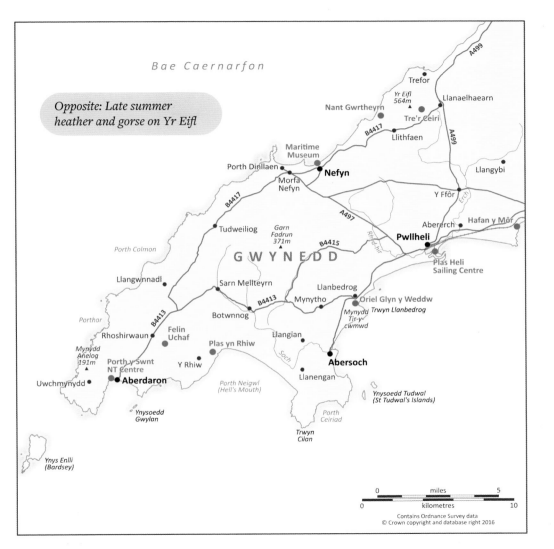

*Opposite: Late summer heather and gorse on Yr Eifl*

First published in 2016

© text:Ioan Roberts

© images:
Cwrw Llŷn merchandise: Dewi Wyn
12-13: N.W. Adventure Activities
Sailing: Plas Heli, Alan Dop, Peter Newton
Gwasg Carreg Gwalch

© publication: Gwasg Carreg Gwalch 2016

ISBN: 978-1-84524-243-5

Cover design: Eleri Owen
Cover image: Tony Jones, Y Rhiw

Published by Gwasg Carreg Gwalch,
12 Iard yr Orsaf, Llanrwst, Wales LL26 0EH
tel: 01492 642031
email: llanrwst@carreg-gwalch.com
website: www.carreg-gwalch.com

# Contents

# Bread and beauty

For the last 60 years, most of Llŷn has been designated an Area of Outstanding Natural Beauty, and few who are familiar with the peninsula would disagree with the description. From early Christian pilgrims to today's walkers, sailors and caravanners, this north western tip of Wales has been an irresistible magnet for visitors. It is also home to a rich cultural heritage, one of a diminishing number of areas in Wales where Cymraeg, is the everyday language of most of the population.

Generations of poets and writers have sought to express the area's beauty in words. A much quoted line by the poet J. Glyn Davies describes Llŷn at the end of day as '*lle i enaid gael llonydd*' – a place to rest the soul. But beneath the tranquillity tensions can arise, and spectacular scenery and magical beaches bring their own challenges. Tourism is the main employer, and plays a vital part in the struggle to provide jobs to keep young people from having to move from the area to find work. But unsuitable developments can damage the things that make the peninsula special to locals and visitors alike. The potential benefit of any planning application has to be balanced against its environmental and cultural impact. Housing schemes, marinas, supermarkets and wind turbines have all come under scrutiny and provoked lively arguments in recent years.

But we are now seeing a new awareness that developing the economy and safeguarding the local heritage and language are not necessarily conflicting aims. Llŷn has become the first area in Wales to embrace the Ecomuseum movement, a concept that originated in France and has spread to many parts of the world. The Llŷn model, called Ecoamgueddfa, works in partnership with diverse organisations that share its vision of celebrating the local identity through community participation. They include a language-learning centre, a maritime museum, an art gallery and a sailing academy. These will be described in later chapters.

At the time of writing (2016) a minibus service, the Llŷn Coastal Bus (01758 721 777; 07974 517 943; oddrwsiddrws @yahoo.co.uk), runs on certain days of the week in the summer from Nefyn to Aberdaron and Abersoch, and provides a

*Porth Dinllaen*

convenient introduction to the area. The hope is that this service will be expanded.

The Llŷn Coastal Path, opened in 2006, is a useful guide for people intent on exploring the area on foot. Stretching for 91 miles (146 km) from Caernarfon to Porthmadog, it forms one of the most scenic parts of the 870-mile (1,400 km) Wales Coast Path. Wales was the first country in the world to provide a dedicated footpath close to most of its coastline. The Llŷn path is divided into seven sections and takes in several secluded coves and cliffs that are inaccessible by car.

The spirit of self-help, with communities taking charge of their own destiny, is not confined to the Ecoamgueddfa organisations. There are several recent examples of new business ventures set up by local people and making use of local produce. These include an award-winning ice cream produced on a family farm in Edern; a renovated bakery with a thatched roof in Aberdaron; pork products on a farm in Llithfaen; and a community-based brewery in Nefyn.

*1. Llanengan; 2. Inner harbour, Abersoch; 3. Felin Uchaf, part of Ecoamgueddfa*

In the 1950s, supporters of a nuclear power station in another rural area in north Wales coined the slogan 'Bread before Beauty'. They were in favour of jobs at any price. People have now come to realise that bread and beauty, with careful planning, can go hand in hand.

# Activities in Llŷn

*A wealth of outdoor activities are offered around the peninsula*

# The oldest rocks on Earth

The name Llŷn, with various spellings, has been recorded in print since the 12th century. A tribal name, Irish in origin, it comes from the same root as *Laighin* or Leinster, the nearest of the four Irish provinces. The older spelling, *Lleyn* no longer has official status, but still appears occasionally.

Llŷn is has not been an administrative unit since the old Llŷn Rural District Council disappeared in a local government reorganisation in the 1970s. Consequently, the eastern boundary of Llŷn is vague and open to interpretation, but on the whole it follows the course of Afon Erch which flows to the sea in Pwllheli harbour.

The Llŷn Coast Path encircles the whole arm that juts out into the Irish Sea all the way from Caernarfon in the north to Porthmadog in the south, and includes communities who would never identify themselves with Llŷn. Some local people on the other hand would consider the tip of the peninsula beyond Nefyn and Pwllheli as the only true Llŷn, or Pen Draw Llŷn (*pen draw:* far end). Cricieth and Clynnog are sometimes referred to as being in Llŷn although Cricieth is technically in Eifionydd and Clynnog in Arfon.

Although the peninsula is low-lying in comparison with the neighbouring Eryri (*Snowdonia*), any cyclist would testify that Llŷn is certainly not flat. As you approach along the A499 from Caernarfon through Clynnog you are confronted by the imposing peaks of Gyrn Goch and Gyrn Ddu to the left and Yr Eifl on the right, the latter bearing the scars of generations of granite quarrying. The road forks just before Llanaelhaearn and after a bit more climbing it's mostly downhill to Nefyn on the northern coast or Pwllheli to the south.

The most prominent landmark further into the peninsula is Garn Fadryn, a steep-sided igneous peak known by geologists as a *monadnock*, which is only 371 metres high but dominates the surrounding countryside. Other hills and headlands in the area have *Mynydd* (mountain) in their names although in other areas they would

*Tre'r Ceiri, one of the three peaks of the Eifl, above Llanaelhaearn*

hardly be high enough to warrant the description. Mynydd Mawr (*mawr*: big) beyond Aberdaron is as far as you can go on the mainland before crossing to Enlli (*Bardsey*). This area consists of rocks from the Pre-Cambrian period, dating from the very beginning of Earth billions of years ago. This ancient landscape was a never-ending source of awe and inspiration to the poet R. S. Thomas when he served as vicar of Aberdaron.

*1. Garn Fadryn;*
*2. Carnguwch - its summit cairn is the largest Bronze Age cairn in Wales;*
*3. Mynydd Anelog*

# Stones and legends

Mynydd Cefnamwlch is a round, bracken-covered hill between Tudweiliog and Llangwnnadl on the north-western coast of Llŷn. At its foot, just off a narrow road to Sarn Mellteyrn, lies Coeten Arthur, one of the oldest surviving man-made structures in the peninsula.

This cromlech, or dolmen, is a burial mound built in the New Stone Age between 4000 and 3000 BC. That was a period of profound change on the land, as hunter-gatherers turned their attention to farming. It was then that our forebears, for reasons unknown, lifted a giant capstone three metres long and one and a half metres wide, and balanced it delicately on top of three supporting stones. Two other boulders now lying nearby could once have formed additional walls to the cromlech. Earth and grass would have covered the structure. The cromlechi were family burial chambers. Some have survived throughout Western Europe, with about 70 still standing in Wales. They are thought to have been in use as burial sites for at least a thousand years, but may have been built to serve some other purpose originally.

The name Coeten Arthur occurs at cromlechi in other parts of Wales, notably Pembrokeshire. 'Coeten' (quoit) was a heavy ring thrown at an upright in an ancient game. According to legend, the cromlech at Cefnamwlch was formed when King Arthur threw the capstone from the top of Garn Fadryn, and his wife carried the three supporting stones to the site in her apron. Arthurian legends probably date from the 5th or 6th centuries AD; so the Coeten Arthur legend could be closer in time to the present day than to the building of the cromlech, which is centuries older than the pyramids of Egypt.

Coeten Arthur is one of several cromlechi and standing stones from roughly the same period that can still be seen around Llŷn. On a farm appropriately called Cromlech near the village of Y Ffôr is a rectangular burial chamber. This had apparently collapsed during the 19th century but was restored in 1936. There are similar structures, less well-preserved,

*1. Cromlech Coeten Arthur;*
*2. Cromlech Y Ffôr; 3. Bach Wen*

at Trwyn Llech y Doll in Cilan and Bryn Parc, Llanbedrog. A cromlech at Fach Wen near Clynnog has more than a hundred marks, known as cupmarks on the capstone. These are now indistinct and their purpose remains a mystery.

Standing stones dotted around the peninsula are a source of intrigue to laymen and professional archaeologists. One of the most striking, at Penfras farm in Llwyndyrys has an unusual, greenish tint (see page 2). But what was it for? A sun dial marking the seasons? Part of a boundary fence? Or did it have religious significance?

In 1956, following a gorse fire on Mynydd Rhiw, a series of holes was noticed in the ground. That was how archaeologists came to discover the site of an important Stone Age axe factory. The site was excavated in the late 1950s and again in 2007. Five round pits were discovered in a row about a hundred yards long, with rubble alongside containing rejected axes. The factory produced small axes for local use and larger ones for cutting trees in other areas. Some of the axes produced on Mynydd Rhiw have been discovered as far away as Herefordshire.

There are several other ancient remains in the Rhiw area, but none more intriguing than what's been described as the oldest brewery in Wales. Archaeological work above Porth Neigwl in 2008 discovered a primitive wooden

trough with a layer of burnt stone. Carbon tests showed that this dated back to the Bronze Age. The remains of barley and wheat were discovered in the trough and it is believed that it was a site for brewing beer. The theory is that our ancestors used to place stones on the bonfire until they became white-hot and then they were carried to the trough to boil the water. The water was then cooled to a temperature of 60 degrees centigrade. A tincture of wheat and barley, flavoured with gorse, heather and herbs was added. Now the cooperative brewery Cwrw Llŷn (See chapter?) have set up Ymddiriedolaeth Porth Neigwl (ymddiriedolaeth:trust), in honour of their predecessors in the trade thousands of years ago.

In the bay beyond Porth Neigwl lies the reef known as Sarn Badrig (*Saint Patrick's Causeway*) which extends from Ynys Enlli towards Harlech. According to legend it was one of the embankments of Cantre'r Gwaelod, a fertile and magical place submerged when drunken watchman Seithennyn left the floodgate open. The earliest record of the story is in a poem in the oldest surviving Welsh manuscript, dating from 1250. Some people believe that the legend is rooted in the folk memory of an actual event. Tree trumps appear in Bae Ceredigion at low tide, and it's known that Wales and Ireland were joined by land been before the end of the Ice Age, around 7,000 BC. Was that land submerged gradually, or was there some catastrophic event that might be known today as a tsunami? Whatever the truth, the memory of Seithennyn is also preserved by the Cwrw Llŷn, who produce a beer that bears his name.

*1. and 2. The 'Porth Neigwl Brewery';*
*3. Sarn Badrig*

# The Celts

It is worth tramping to the summit of Tre'r Ceiri, the most easterly of the three peaks of Yr Eifl, for the view alone, a panorama that can extend on a clear day from the Wicklow Mountains in Ireland past the grandeur of Eryri to the distant Preseli Mountains in Pembrokeshire. But the main most rewarding aspect of the trek is the Iron Age fort under your feet, 'the most impressive and dramatic of all British hillforts' according to archaeologist James Dyer, who excavated the site in 1904. Around two thousand such forts have survived throughout Britain.

The site occupies five acres of land, surrounded by a defensive wall over 3 metres high in places. You can see the bases of 150 round huts that would once have been roofed with straw or heather, and had enough space for a population of up to 500 people. The site is believed to have been occupied from around 200 BC until the end of the Roman period. The occupants would now be classified as Celts, a term broadly applied to the language, art and artefacts of Iron Age Peoples.

But why build houses 500 metres above sea level when there is ample space on lower ground? This settlement would be classifies as a bryngaer = *'fort on the hill'* – which implies a military purpose, and any aspiring aggressor would have been spotted miles away. But there is no evidence of warfare at Tre'r Ceiri and some archaeologists believe that the early settlers may have been drawn to the site by the same breath-taking scenery that attracts people here today. Others maintain that Tre'r Ceiri was part of a *'hafod'* and *'hendref'* system, where shepherds would spend the summer months tending their sheep from the upland *'hafod'* before descending to the 'hendref' for the winter. Any remains of a 'hendref' at the foot of Yr Eifl could have been obliterated by centuries of farming. In the early 1990s Tre'r Ceiri was researched and carefully repaired by the Gwynedd Archaeological Trust. Some misplaced stones were put back in their original location, and a lintel which had snapped in half was repaired and replaced above one of the entrances.

Yr Eifl's other peaks are Garn Ganol

*Fort wall and hut circles at Tre'r Ceiri*

and Garn Fôr. They are sometimes wrongly referred to in English as 'The Rivals'. The name is a mutation of *geifl*, the plural of *gafl* meaning *fork*.

The earliest hill fort in Llŷn is probably Castell Odo on Mynydd yr Ystum in Rhoshirwaun, believed to date from the Bronze Age (2500-600 BC). Evidence suggests that the fort was attacked by the Romans who burnt all the timber before allowing the residents to return. Nearby there is a large stone called Carreg Samson with five recesses said to represent Samson's finger marks when the giant threw the boulder from the summit of Mynydd Enlli. The old Celts were obviously adept at throwing stones. It's said that there is a pot of gold buried under Carreg Samson, and that any attempt to move the stone to look for it would cause the biggest thunderstorm ever seen.

Garn Boduan, near Nefyn, has remains of 150 round huts similar to those on Tre'r Ceiri. They are known locally as Cytiau Gwyddelod which means 'huts of the Irish'. No evidence survives of any direct links with Ireland, but the name could stem from folk memories of raids from the west around the end of the Roman occupation. Yet another hillfort can be seen on Garn Fadryn, which also has 'Cytiau Gwyddelod' on its summit, as well as the remains of a medieval castle built by the sons of Owain Gwynedd, the first person to hold the title Prince of Wales.

The language spoken within hillforts was Brythoneg, the Celtic language spoken throughout most of Britain during the Iron Age and Roman period. Over the centuries this evolved into two families, Q Celtic, spoken in Wales, Britany and Cornwall, and P Celtic, the language of Scotland, Ireland and the Isle of Man. It's a sobering thought that the language spoken by the inhabitants of Tre'r Ceiri thousands of years ago might not have been all that different from that spoken in the surrounding countryside today.

1. *Castell Odo; 2. Garn Boduan round huts, with Garn Fadryn in the distance*

# The Age of Saints

The fact that there are around 650 towns and villages in Wales whose names begin with 'Llan', and that this is usually followed by the name of a saint, is an indication of the importance of the Age of Saints in Welsh history. Oes y Seintiau is the name given to the period from about the 4th to the 8th century when Christianity was introduced throughout the land by roving monks and missionaries who later became known as saints. They were not all evangelical preachers. Some were hermits in search of mental and spiritual peace.

'Llan' originally meant an enclosed piece of land. Then a religious cell would be established on the land, followed by the building of a church or monastery, so that 'llan' became the word for 'church'. As a cluster of houses was built around the site, the name of the church and saint would become the name of the village. 'Lan' which occurs in Breton and Cornish place-names has the same origin.

The lives of the saints have been chronicled in *Bucheddau'r Saint* (*bucheddau*: lives), written in the Middle Ages, although the authors appeared to be more concerned with heaping praise on the subjects than with stating facts. The heroes were portrayed as having supernatural powers that were not always put to Christian use. Beuno, the most influential saint in northern Wales, is said to have planted a magic tree by his father's grave in Montgomeryshire, a tree that would kill any Englishman who passed underneath but would let any Welsh person safely by! But Beuno, we are told, also used to feed and clothe the needy and visit the sick and imprisoned. Beuno is the patron saint of churches at Clynnog Fawr, Deneio (Pwllheli), Pistyll, Carnguwch and Botwnnog.

Pilgrimages became popular throughout western Europe in medieval times. Whereas the better-off would visit Rome, Jerusalem or Canterbury, the main destinations in Wales were Tyddewi (*St David's*), Treffynnon (*Holywell*) and Ynys Enlli. There were northern and southern routes on the Pilgrims' Trail to Enlli through Llŷn, and most of the churches

*1. Clynnog Fawr; 2. Cyff Beuno – the saint's 'chest'; 3. Maen Beuno*

survive, part of an unbroken tradition dating back to early Christianity.

Recently there has been renewed interest in following the footsteps trail of these early pilgrims. A formal pilgrimage was organised by the Bishop of Bangor in 1950, and his successor led another one that drew hundreds of people in 1992. There are now slate signs signifying parts of the Pilgrims' Trail. Modern day pilgrims may not always share the motivations of their forebears, but the peace and tranquillity of these ancient churches transcends the centuries.

As its full name, Clynnog Fawr yn Arfon, implies, the village of Clynnog is outside the boundaries of Llŷn, but a visit to St Beuno's church is essential for anyone interested in the story of the pilgrims. The size and majestic architecture of the building is an indication of its former importance: it is said that it was a visit to this church that prompted Sir Clough Williams-Ellis, creator of Portmeirion Italian village, to become an architect. Inside the building, 1350 years of Christian activity are vividly portrayed in its features and explained in concise information panels.

The present church was built in the 16th century on the site of an earlier one established by St Beuno around 616 AD on land gifted to him by the kings of Gwynedd. Even earlier a well, 200 yards from the church on the road to Pwllheli, was being used to christen children and provide refreshment for pilgrims. More recently, sick children would be soaked in the well and laid to rest overnight on a bed of reeds on top of Beuno's grave in the church, and would wake up cured of their ailment. The grave in Beuno's Cell can still be seen.

In the saint's day, according to legend, you could walk at low tide from Clynnog Fawr to Clynnog Fach on Anglesey. When Beuno was on his way to Anglesey to preach, he accidentally dropped his book of sermons in the water. A passing curlew retrieved the book in its beak and gave it back to him. Beuno repaid the favour by ensuring that a curlew's nest, forever after, would be hard to find.

It was in Capel Beuno within the church that poet and critic Eben Fardd established a school in the 19th century.

This was later transferred to his home and then to a purpose-built school building, which has just been renovated by Canolfan Hanes Uwchgwyrfai, a recently-formed history and heritage society.

*1. Eglwys Carnguwch; 2. Eglwys Pistyll; 3. Standing stone in Sarn Mellteyrn churchyard*

# Other places of worship

In Llŷn as in many other places, life is becoming more secular and many churches and chapels are closing their doors. Yet there is still interest in the Christian heritage central to the story of the peninsula. This chapter takes a random look at some sites that are part of this story.

Aelhaearn was a disciple of Beuno, and like his master, had his family roots in Montgomeryshire, mid Wales. He established the first church at **Llanaelhaearn** in the 7th century. The present building is in the form of a cross and divided into three parts: chancel, sanctuary and nave. One wall has a stone with the Latin inscription, *'Aliortvs Elmatiacos hic iacet'* - 'here lays Aliortus, of Elfed'. Elfed was the name of a Brythonic kingdom near present-day Leeds. It is not far from Catterick, or Catraeth, site of a battle between Celts and Romans which inspired the earliest surviving Welsh poetry. Aliortus may have been part of a Christian migration from that area to Wales.

**Carnguwch** and **Pistyll**, two other churches with 7th century roots and dedicated to Beuno, are among the smallest that the pilgrims would have visited on their way to Enlli. Carnguwch, on a secluded spot above Afon Erch, is a sturdy building with a square bell tower. The building had been in decline until it was tastefully repaired recently by local volunteers.

**Pistyll** church nestles on the bank of a stream between the village and the sea. A small, atmospheric building with a covering of straw on the floor and herbs decorating the walls and windows, it evokes a strong sense of the past. Near the altar there is a 'lepers' window', where the unfortunate victims could watch from the outside as the priest served communion. A wall by the roadside in Pistyll has an ancient stone bearing a Celtic cross, believed to be the gravestone of a saint or pilgrim.

The church at **Llanengan**, the centre of the large parish that contains Abersoch, would have been on the southerly path to

*Llanaelhaearn church*

Enlli. Its patron saint, Engan or Einion, was one of the three founders of the monastery on the island. Much of the present building of St Einion's church, with its square tower, three bells and arched windows, dates from the end of the 15th century. The bells, a screen and an oak chest that used to house the church treasures are thought to have come from the St Mary's monastery on Enlli. The chest was carved from a single piece of wood and originally had three locks with a key each given to the vicar and two church wardens.

At the western end of the church a weekly school was held for a period in the 18th century, with the help of one of Wales' best-known educators. Griffith Jones, rector of Llanddowror near Carmarthen, is remembered for the circulating schools he set up, where children and adults would attend school in one location for three months at a time and taught to read the Bible and the catechism before the school moved somewhere else. This made a huge contribution towards making the country literate. And it was Griffith Jones who paid the wages of a teacher who taught the scripture and general knowledge at the church in Llanengan.

In the church cemetery at neighbouring village **Llangïan**, there is a memorial stone dating from the 5th or 6th century bearing the Latin words *'Meli Medici Fili Martini Jacit'* – 'Here lies Meli the Doctor, Son of Martinus'. The identity of Meli is unknown, but this is the only tombstone from that period in Wales and England to specify that the person buried was a doctor by profession.

There is another interesting church at **Llanfihangel Bachellaeth** – 'the quietest place in Llŷn' according to Pwllheli-born poet Cynan. It's located in a maze of winding lanes between Nanhoron, Mynytho and Rhydyclafdy. The church ceased being a place of regular worship at the beginning of the 20th century and has been deconsecrated and sold to a private owner. Many of its artefacts have disappeared and a mounting stone on top of which the Methodist evangelist Howel Harris is said to have preached towards the

*1. Font at Llanengan; 2. Screen at Llanengan; 3. Llangïan stone; 4. Llanfihangel Bachellaeth?*

end of the 17th century has been relocated outside the chapel at Rhydyclafdy.

**Llangwnnadl** has one of the best-preserved churches in Llŷn. St Gwynhoedl, its 6th century founder, was one of the earliest monks to work on the peninsula. The first thing you notice is the ornate iron gate incorporating a Celtic cross and the word *'Tŷ Dduw'* (house of God), a gift from William Jones, Aberdaron's last blacksmith, in the 1960s. The pews and other woodwork were renovated around the same time.

The oldest part of the present building, the central of its three sections, dates from the 15th century. A field above the church is still known as Cae Eisteddfa – 'place to sit' – where pilgrims could rest before embarking on the final stage of their journey.

St Hywyn's church in **Aberdaron** is a majestic building right on the seashore. At one time the sea was eroding the churchyard to such an extent that the parishioners built another church in 1841, further inland. Then they returned to the original building, protected by a new sea defence wall. The interior of the church was extensively restored recently following an appeal for £20,000.

The earliest church on the site was built in the 6th century and some of the present walls date from the Middle Ages. Gruffudd ap Cynan, king of Gwynedd, was given refuge by the monks during his conflict with the Normans, before he fled to Ireland. Some years later his son-in-law, Gruffudd ap Rhys, Prince of Deheubarth, received the same favour in Aberdaron after falling out with none other than his father-in-law.

It was in a building belonging to the church that the leader of the Welsh revolt, Owain Glyndŵr, held a secret meeting in 1405 with his son-in-law Edward Mortimer and Henry Percy, Earl of Northumberland. The plan was to establish a tripartite agreement that would share England and Wales between the three, with Owain's Cymru including a large slice of present-day England.

The final resting place for many pilgrims before the passage to Enlli would have been Ffynnon Fair, the holy well at the foot of the headland directly opposite the island. Not easy to find and inaccessible at high tide, it's been credited with healing powers. Part of its mystique stems from a common belief that its water is always pure although it gets submerged by the sea at hight tide. But a recent writer, Jim Perrin, says that this is a myth spread by the 'normally reliable' antiquarian Thomas Pennant in 1783 and that Ffynnon Fair is actually 10 feet above high water.

Nonconformity, although now in sharp decline, has long been the dominant religion in Llŷn. In **Nanhoron** lies Capel Newydd (*new chapel*), which is ironically the oldest nonconformist place of worship still standing in northern Wales. Described by the poet Cynan as a small, whitewashed chapel in the far end of Llŷn, it was built in 1769 on the Nanhoron Estate and with the support of the Lady of the Manor, Catherine Edwards. Unusually for her class, she had deserted the Anglican faith and joined the Independent denomination because of the kindness shown to her by Nonconformists after her soldier husband died on a ship on his way home from war in the West Indies.

The building was declining rapidly until the 1950s, when local people came together to restore it to its original condition. Today it is in the care of conservation agency CADW.

*Capel Newydd, Nanhoron*

# Isle of Saints and Sinners

Enlli (*Bardsey*) means island in the currents, and even on a calm day the tides can make the Swnt (*Sound*) hazardous for all but the most competent sailors. The nearest cemetery on the mainland contains ample evidence of past tragedies. Despite the vast improvements in boats and their powerful engines, any visitors to the island are made aware that their stay might last longer than they intended.

Not everyone who was lured to live on the island in the past led saintly lives. Pirates and smugglers as well as fishermen and farmers can be listed among former residents. But it is the unbroken Christian tradition above all else that gives the island a special place in the history of Wales.

The main architect of that tradition was Cadfan, a Breton-born missionary commemorated in several places in Wales. He had previously lived in a monastic community at Tywyn in Meirionnydd and was captivated by the sight of this dream island across the ocean. He sailed across and established a monastery on the island around 515 AD. According to Geraldus Cambrensis, an early travel writer who called by in 1188, nobody ever died of illness on Enlli, only of old age. That may have contributed to the legend that 20,000 saints are buried there. By medieval times the island had become a busy destination for pilgrims, and the Pope ruled that three pilgrimages to Enlli were equivalent to one to Rome. The earliest surviving relics on the island are the tower of a 13th century abbey and the adjacent remnants of an older cross. The abbey was closed in 1537 during the Protestant Reformation and the Dissolution of the Monasteries.

In the 16th century it was mostly pirates, rather than holy men, who ruled the island. They were motivated by greed rather than necessity. Many of these were well-off landowners including the infamous John Wyn ap Huw of Bodfel, who had been given the island as a gift but still hankered after more wealth. This was a far from tranquil time on the Island of Saints.

*1. Enlli from Mynydd Mawr;*
*2. Early Christian stones; 3. The Chapel*

3

By the end of the 18th century order had been restored, with the islanders again earning an honest living through farming and fishing. There were then about 80 people living in the island's 12 to 15 homes. Part of their work involved sailing or rowing all the way to Liverpool to sell their produce. The year 1821 saw the building of the lighthouse, with its unusual square tower. In the last century the population went into steep decline. There was a major exodus in 1925, the school closed in 1947, the last minister departed, and soon afterwards the native families left one by one.

In common with some islands off the Scottish and Irish coast, a senior member of the community was elevated to 'King' of the island. 'Brenin Enlli' wore a brass crown provided by the island's owners, the Newborough estate, and on his death the title would pass on to his son. The last king of Enlli was Love Pritchard who died in 1927. The crown can now be seen at the Liverpool Maritime Museum, although there have been calls to relocate it nearer its home.

Enlli was an inspiration for many Welsh-language poets, as well as English-language work by R.S.Thomas, who was a frequent visitor, and Christine Evans who lives on the island for part of the year. The artist Brenda Chamberlain lived on Enlli from 1947 to 1962 and some of her pictures can still be seen in one of the farmhouses. More recently, the photographer Marian Delyth became a regular visitor and some of her stunning photographs are featured in her book *Enlli – tu hwnt I'r Swnt*.

Since 1979 the island is owned by a trust, Ymddiriedolaeth Ynys Enlli, and administered in partnership with the Countryside Commission and CADW. Daily visits are run from Porth Meudwy and occasionally from Pwllheli. The journey takes around an hour, and allows day visitors a few hours on the island. Nine houses are used to accommodate visitors.

Enlli has been designated a National Nature Reserve and a Site of Special Scientific Interest. Although visitors are welcome, their numbers are controlled so as not to ruin the character and environment of the island. Farming is

1. *'The King of Bardsey'; 2. A typical island dwelling; 3. Y Cafn - the harbour*

conducted in a manner that sustains the wild life. No commercial fertilisers are used and the cattle and sheep stock are carefully bred and maintained. Native trees such as hawthorn and elder are encouraged, and imported fuschia and evergreens have been uprooted. Grey seals breed in the surrounding rocks.. Among the rare flowers growing on the island is the spring squil.

Enlli has fascinated bird watchers for many years. In 1953 the Bardsey Bird & Field Observatory was established in one of the farmhouses. More than 300 species of birds have been recorded on the island, including red-legged crows, oystercatchers and Manx shearwaters

New treasures are still being discovered on Enlli. In September 2000, a visitor noticed unusual features in an apple growing on a gnarled old tree, and consulted the experts. Afal Enlli is now an official name for the rarest apple variety in the world, believed to have been grown in a monastery orchard on the island one thousand years ago.

The Enlli lighthouse, built in 1821, is the only one run by Trinity House in the UK to have a square tower. It is also one of the highestat 30 metres (98 feet).The lighthouse-keepers always played an important part in the life of Enlli the island and the islanders were often more fluent in English than their contemporaries on the mainland. It was the end of an era in 1987 when the lighthouse went automatic. In 2014 the lighthouse lens was removed and can now be seen outside Porth y Swnt, the National Trust's Visitor Centre in Aberdaron.

*1. The island's old school; 2. The lighthouse; 3. Porth y Swnt, Aberdaron*

# Princes of Wales

With the Wicklow Mountains near enough to be clearly visible from parts of Llŷn on a clear day, it is little wonder that connections with Ireland, whether for trade, religion or plunder, are an integral part of the history and heritage of Llŷn. The western seaboard of Europe was a busy highway in the days when it was easier to travel by sea than by land.

The foundations of Castell Einion on Mynydd Cilan above Porth Neigwl are related to the history of a Bythonic tribe which moved from southern Scotland to Gwynedd in the 5th century, to secure the region agains invading Irishmen. The leader was Cunedda and one of his great-grandsons was Einion (founder of Llanengan) and the King of Llŷn with his westward looking castle on Cilan.

One regular travellers across the Irish Sea was Gruffudd ap Cynan, King of Gwynedd, who had close family links on both sides.

Gruffudd was born in 1055 in Ireland, where his Welsh father was king-in-exile of Gwynedd, having been ousted from his throne through devious by his Norman enemies. Gruffudd's mother was the daughter of a Dublin king of Scandinavian origin. On his father's death the young Gruffudd came to Wales with a group of followers to try and regain his heritage, but having won battles in Llŷn and Meirionnydd, he was defeated at Clynnog by Trahaearn, an impostor who had claimed the family's throne. Gruffudd's cause was not helped by a rift that developed between his supporters in Llŷn and Scandinavians who had come over from Ireland to fight on his behalf. Gruffudd had to flee back to the land of his birth.

In 1081 he landed in Dyfed, and helped his friend, Rhys ap Tewdwr, to regain the throne of Deheubarth. But although his adversary Trahaearn was killed in battle, Gruffudd was betrayed by Meirion Goch, who lived in Castellmarch, Abersoch. He had invited Gruffudd to Rhug near Corwen to meet two Norman leaders, the Earls of Chester and Shrewsbury, to negotiate a peaceful settlement. The Normans had virtually conquered England in one battle in 1066, but were mountainous terrain and fractious nature of the Welsh more of a challenge. When Gruffudd and a band of

*Llanengan church, founded by king Einion*

friends arrived in Rhug, the Normans were not there to talk peace. They cut off the right thumbs of his followers before releasing them, and imprisoned Gruffudd in Chester. He escaped after 12 years in captivity and lived on the run. Eventually he made his way to Aberdaron and sailed to Ireland with the help of monks from Ynys Enlli.

He assembled a fleet of 23 ships and returned again to Wales to confront the Huw Flaidd, Earl of Chester. This time he got enthusiastic support from Llŷn ac Eifionydd and with his allies in Deheubarth kept the Normans at bay, inspiring one of the most unified and productive periods in the nation's history. The invaders were defeated and north and south-western Wales were rid of Normans for a generation.

Gruffudd ap Cynan held the title Prince of Wales, the first of a number of Welsh Princes who ruled the country in Medieval times. Their era came to an end with the killing in 1282 of Llywelyn ap Gruffudd, known as Llywelyn Ein Llyw Olaf (*llyw*: ruler; *olaf*: last) at Cilmeri near Builth Wells.

Nefyn and Pwllheli had a long history as administrative centres before the conquest of Wales. Nefyn is mentioned in documents from the late 11th century as a landing place for Gruffudd ap Cynan, who was given sanctuary in the church. It had a motte and bailey castle and was one of the main headquarters of the Princes of Gwynedd. After the conquest it became a royal borough and a centre for collecting taxes and debts. By 1293 there were 93 ratepayers in Nefyn including tradesmen, a goldsmith, a publican and a priest. About half the population owned fishing net or a boat.

The victorious King Edward I marked his victory with a tour of his new found territories, and commissioned an inventory of the properties. Of the two towns in Llŷn, Nefyn, with 121 families, was considerably larger than Pwllheli, with 21. It was some time later that Pwllheli outgrew its rival. When Edward visited Nefyn in 1284 to celebrate his conquest, there were so many revellers at the feast that the floor collapsed under their feet. The field where a tournament was held as part of the festivities is still known as Cae Iorwerth – Edward's field.

*The church and bay of Aberdaron*

Nefyn was burned to the ground in around 1400 by the forces of Welsh rebel-prince Owain Glyndŵr who was set on restoring Welsh independence. This was Nefyn's punishment for its links with the English crown, and it took a long time to recover. The first official reference to Pwllheli dates from the period of Edward's conquest, but there is evidence the town had already existed for centuries. Pwllheli's leading historian D. G. Lloyd Hughes believed that the Pen-y-mownt area of the town was so named because it was the site of a motte-and-bailey castle. The Welsh princes built these from the middle of the 12th century under the influence of the Normans, usually at the site of the prince's court. The court at Pwllheli could have been sited originally where a farmhouse called Henllys (*hen*: old; *llys*: court) still stands on a hill above the town, with another one built later at the Pen-y-mownt. A pile of soil found nearby could have been remains of the mound of the castle. The name Gadlys in the same part of town adds weight to this theory.

Pwllheli too paid a price for receiving favours from the English Crown, and was attacked by Owain Glyndŵr's forces with its entire population forced to flee. Glyndŵr's dream of political and religious independence struck a chord with a high proportion of his compatriots. The first decade of the 15th century was arguably the most united period in Welsh history. But his influence waned as the Crown tightened its grip, and by the end of the decade the uprising was virtually over. Owain died around 1415. His burial place was never disclosed, and he was never betrayed by any of his followers.

In Pwllheli as elsewhere, poverty and anarchy were the immediate outcome of the rebellion, and order was not restored until the end of the century. But that tempestuous decade rekindled the national spirit and some would argue that its effect is still evident today.

*A celebration of Welsh flags on Pwllheli's main streets today*

# Harvesting the sea

According to Ward Lock's *Travel Guide to Pwllheli and North Wales*, published in the 1940s, the name of the town 'is a corruption of Porth Heli, the port of one Heli, who was lord of the district'. It's an interesting story, without a grain of truth. The name, meaning 'salt water pool', originated in a soggy piece of land that used to be washed over by sea water at high tide, located where the Asda supermarket now stands. A local eisteddfod in the Victorian era were set the task of devising an English name for the town. One competitor, aghast at the idea, suggested Salt Lake City. Fishermen and their families in that area were probably among the first people to settle in Pwllheli. The inventory of King Edward's new-found possessions after the conquest noted that Pwllheli had two boats and several fishing nets. That figure was not necessarily accurate, as the purpose of the exercise was taxation.

Over the next centuries Pwllheli evolved as a port and commercial centre, with a thriving shipbuilding industry, described in another chapter. Even before the harbour was built, it was a natural haven for ships, and a convenient place for trading with Western Europe. Herring, lobsters and crabs were exported, and salt for their preservation became an important commodity. By the end of the 19th century large boats from further afield began to enter the harbour and fish stocks started to decline, possibly through overfishing.

The sea was traditionally an important source of livelihood in Nefyn, although many of the fishermen had other jobs as well. The sheltered bay was an ideal anchorage for merchant ships, and three herrings on the town's coat of arms leave no doubt as to the main harvest. The booming herring industry made the town famous, and according to a local saying, Nefyn herrings had 'backs like farmers and bellies like publicans'. Residents of the town are still sometimes referred to as Penwaig Nefyn (penwaig: herring). The name Tŷ Halen (halen: salt) on a house near the town centre is a reminder of the importance of salt for preserving the fish. Herring stocks declined seriously during

*1. A fishing boat entering Pwllheli harbour;*
*2. Porth Ysgaden*

the 20th century and the industry has almost disappeared. The story of those tempestuous days is told at the Llŷn Maritime Museum, described later.

Few people in the peninsula now earn their living entirely from fishing, although a co-operative venture, Cymdeithas Pysgotwyr Llŷn, has been established to boost the industry. But many people still set their lobster pots, and anchor their boats in various bays and coves around the peninsula.

The fact that these little coves are known as porth (port) is an indication of their past roles. Horse-drawn carts would trundle to deliver farm produce to sailing ships, or to collect coal and lime and other goods. The unloading of coal from one of the larger ships at Porth Colmon in Llangwnnadl was a social occasion that could take a couple of days. In Porth Ysgaden, Tudweiliog, lime carried ashore would be burned in a kiln near the beach. The gable end of a ruined house still stands guard above the shore; one family who lived in it used to place candles or lamps in their window as a warning to ships on stormy nights.

It was from Porth Fesyg further west that three brothers from Rhoshirwaun went out in a boat in June 1933 to set lobster pots, defying the stormy conditions. Their bodies were discovered over the next few days, and one of Wales' best poets R. Williams Parry composed a verse which is inscribed on their gravestone.

At Easter 1933, two young fishermen from Tudweiliog ventured out from Porth Ysgaden in a tiny boat to check their lobster pots. They too were caught in a storm, lost an oar and were blown out to sea, but their story had a happy ending. After drifting for two days they struck land in Kilkeel in Northern Ireland where they were accommodated for the night in the blacksmith's house.

Few people in the area now earn their living entirely from fishing, although a co-operative venture, Cymdeithas Pysgotwyr Llŷn, has been established to boost the industry. But many people still set their lobster pots, and local restaurants and hotels are putting more emphasis on local produce.

In 2012 there was strong opposition in coastal areas throughout Wales when the

*1. An old postcard of Nefyn fishermen; 2. A Llŷn lobster; 3. A Llŷn fisherman*

Welsh Government announced a plan to set up 10 marine conservation zones. These would have introduced stringent restrictions on fishing rights in order to protect dwindling stocks. One zone would have covered the sea around Aberdaron and Ynys Enlli which infuriated local fishermen fearful for their livelihood. Led by Colin Evans, whose family had fished in the area for generations, they played a leading paart in the Wales-wide opposition to the plan. They took their fight to the Welsh Assembly where Colin Evans said that if he couldn't fish in the future he would be unlikely to carry on with other aspects of his work, such as ferrying tourists and carrying supplies for the island's residents. The fishermen were all in favour of marine conservation, he argued: 'Sustainable pot fishermen like us are the only conservationists who have a proven track record in this area.'

A year later the Welsh Government performed a U-turn and withdrew the plan. And Colin Evans still sets his lobster pots around Ynys Enlli.

*1. Porth Nefyn; 2. Fishermen trailers at Porth Dinllaen; 3. Porth Meudwy*

# Wealth from the rocks

Llŷn is not usually associated with heavy industry, but not so long ago quarrying and mining was a major source of employment in parts of the peninsula. The granite quarries around Llithfaen, Trefor and Llanaelhaearn were the biggest in the world. Further into the peninsula hundreds of men dug for copper, lead and manganese in the areas around Abersoch and Rhiw.

The curiously shaped rump of Carreg yr Imbill – 'Gimlet Rock' – at the southern edge of the beach in Pwllheli is a monument to what was once the town's major industry. Old photographs show this as a majestic landmark that was useful as a navigation aid for sailors. Quarrying began around 1814 and accelerated with the establishment of the Liverpool and Pwllheli Granite Company in 1857. There were concerns from the outset about the effect of the quarrying on the landscape. A poem written by Eben Fardd in 1857 predicts that the rock's disappearance would deprive the traeth (beach) of its beauty.

The quarry produced setts, mainly to pave the streets of English cities. Early in the life of the new company orders were secured from Canada and the United States, and a quay was built nearby for loading ships. After that the quarry's fortunes fluctuated, reaching its zenith in the years immediately before the Great War. The lease, and with it the life of the quarry, expired at the beginning of the Second World War.

Graphic tales of life in the quarries of Yr Eifl are told in the autobiography of Griffith R. Williams of Llithfaen, written in 1990 when he was 101 years old. His career in the quarry lasted unbroken from his apprenticeship at the age of 13 to his retirement aged 71. Life was hard and hazardous on the rock face and yet he only witnessed three fatal accidents. But he only narrowly escaped being a victim himself after plunging to the bottom of the sea from a ship that was being loaded. He says: 'A big Irish lad jumped after me... he grabbed my coat and pulled me up like a bear tugging a cat. They gave him a gold watch for saving my life but he sold it to buy drink.'

The scars in the cliffs above the village

*Eifl granite quarrymen*

of Trefor provide dramatic evidence of the hustle and bustle of the old days. The appropriately named Gwaith Mawr (gwaith: works) was once the largest granite quarry in the world. The setts paved the streets of Liverpool, Manchester, Dublin and cities throughout the world.

It was the quarries that created Trefor, which developed into a busy port. Workers and their families arrived from Ireland, England and beyond, and became Welsh in no time. Some of their surnames survive in local families. A strong cultural and musical tradition developed around the quarries, and Trefor's silver band, established in 1863, has won wide acclaim.

The granite industry also created the remote, picturesque, busy but short-lived coastal settlement of Nant Gwrtheyrn. Granite was first mined there around the middle of the 19th century when industrial cities were expanding rapidly. 'Barracks' were erected to accommodate incoming Irish workers, and stone houses were built later for families. The market declined in the 20th century and the work virtually collapsed during the Second World War.

The last families left Nant Gwrtheyrn soon afterwards. Nant Gwrtheyrn is now a flourishing language-learning centre, as we'll see later.

A few quarrymen are still employed in Trefor, and curling stones made from Eifl granite were used in the Winter Olympics of 2006.

Some believe that mining in the Llanengan area near Abersoch goes back to Roman times, but evidence is scarce. According to John Bennett and Robert Vernon, authors of Metal Mines of Llanengan (Gwydyr Mines Publications, 2003) the earliest record of mining is found in letters written in 1638 by Thomas Bushell, seeking permission to mine silver for a new royal mint he had set up in Aberystwyth castle. That venture was short-lived, and subsequent mining projects in Llanengan and Bwlchtocyn were sporadic and generally none too successful.

One owner found the going so hard that he had to pay his men in potatoes instead of money! Another decided there was no substitute for experience and recruited tin workers from Cornwall to try and reverse his fortunes. A plaque

*1. Nant Gwrtheyrn; 2. The quarrymen remembered; 3. Carreg yr Imbill quarrymen*

commemorates Cornish Row, the now demolished houses where the incomers lived on Penrhyn Du. Pumping water from the mines was expensive, the geology challenging, the markets uncertain. Yet the industry kept expanding and employed 300 workers in its heyday in the 1870s.

A jetty was built at the foot of Penrhyn Du to load and unload ships, with a tramline from there to Llanengan. The bed of the tramline is still visible, and some of the company buildings form part of the Porth Tocyn Hotel.

As with all mining, it was a hazardous occupation. The most serious accident occurred in 1885 when three workers drowned after the shaft where they were working was flooded with water from an adjoining shaft. Safety inspectors' investigation showed that company bosses had miss-calculated the relative positions of the two shafts. John Hughes, William Ellis and Owen Jones paid with their lives, and the mine owner and his manager got away with a £20 fine.

Today most of the shafts have disappeared and only those familiar with the site can recognise other evidence of the activity. But the ventilation shaft was renovated at the end of the 1990s and stands as a proud monument to an exciting chapter in the history of the parish of Llanengan.

Porth Ysgo near Rhiw still bears the scars of open-cast manganese mining. Manganese, used mainly in steel manufacture, was first mined in the Rhiw area in 1886. Production reached its peak during the First World War due to the demands of the Arms industry, the activity ceased in the 1920s, enjoyed a brief revival at the start of World War 2 before their final demise.

Jasper, a red stone used for decorative purposes in the building industry was quarried in the early 20th century at Mynydd Carreg near Aberdaron. There were plans to build a jetty at nearby Porthor to transport the products by ship, but that scheme never materialised. Instead, Jasper from Carreg was transported by lorry to various destinations, and still lines the walls of iconic buildings in London.

One ambitious plan to exploit the mineral wealth of the peninsula never came to fruition. The Rhoshirwaun Coal

*1. Porth Ysgo; 2. Llanengan chimney*

Mining Company was set up in the late 19th century. Details are sketchy, but Llŷn could have looked a very different place if a coalmine had been developed in one of its quietest parts.

# Ships Ahoy

Bryn Hyfryd is a substantial house at the town end of Lôn Abererch in Pwllheli. This was the home of William Jones the Druggist, a successful businessman who became the most important of Pwllheli's shipbuilders. William Jones was also religious, a devout Baptist. The night before one of his ships, the William Carey, was launched in 1848 he insisted that its crew of 25 attended a seiat (prayer meeting) in Capel Penmownt to seek blessing for the new vessel. But other men in the town felt aggrieved because they had been refused a job on the ship. They adjourned to a pub for an alternative meeting. That revelry entered the town's folklore and is still remembered as Noson y Seiat Feddw – the night of the drunken seiat.

Small single mast ships were built on beaches in Llŷn throughout the 18th century, mostly for conveying farm produce along the local coast. What boosted the industry and provided an opportunity for entrepreneurs like William Jones was the rapid growth of slate quarries in Snowdonia and Meirionnydd. Small ships were no longer sufficient. Ports such as Porthmadog and Felinheli required sturdy vessels that could withstand the rigours of Cape Horn and the North Sea. Shipyards were established at Pwllheli to meet the demand.

Between 1759 and 1878 more than 400 ships were built, originally near Penmownt and Y Traeth, and later at Glandon and the base of Allt Fawr, between Lôn Abererch and Lôn Caernarfon. The timber came from Meirionnydd in the early days, and then had to be imported from Canada. Pwllheli became one of the most important shipbuilding centres in Wales. Launching a ship was a major event and the town's schools closed for the day.

The largest ship built at Pwllheli was the 693 ton barque Margaret Pugh, and one of the most famous was the Theda, a 150 ton schooner which broke a record by sailing from Labrador to Gibraltar in 12 days. The industry reached its peak in 1840, with 28 ships built and 14 launched in Pwllheli during the year.

In the early days the work was supervised by men from Liverpool, but

*An old timber yard on the quay at Pwllheli*

local craftsmen soon mastered the skills. And businessmen like William Jones who developed the yards showed none of the lack of enterprise sometimes attributed to the Welsh. This was a thoroughly Welsh industry, and local poets would compose short stanzas or englynion to paint on a ship's bow.

It was advancements in technology that brought about the demise of the industry. The railway provided a more convenient means of transporting slates, steam displaced sail, steel ships replaced wooden ones, and small ports like Porthmadog went into decline. The last two ships built at Pwllheli were completed in 1878.

Pwllheli's sailors had shown immense skills and courage all over the world. But there were hazards in home waters as well, notably Sarn Badrig. At the end of the 19th century a famous lifeboat designer called Henry Richardson came to live in Bryn Hyfryd, the old home of William Jones the Druggist. When Richardson died, one of his lifeboats, an open rowing boat, was presented to the town, and a shed erected to store it. This was the start of the lifeboat service, still an important part of the town's life.

From the early 19th century, Nefyn another too was an important shipbuilding centre. The beach became a hive of activity; craftsmen would walk there from adjoining villages to find work and families from further afield moved to live in the area. Wooden ships were built, repaired and enlarged. Nefyn ships built mostly of solid oak were renowned for their strength and seaworthiness rather than their looks. In the heyday of sail between 1760 and 1880, 120 ships were built at Nefyn.

Nearby Porth Dinllaen was also an important shipbuilding centre and port. Fifty-seven ships were built there between 1776 and 1876. Many did not come back from their adventures around the world. The last ship built at Porth Dinllaen, the Annie Lloyd, sank in the Bahamas in 1907.

*Ship building at Porth Nefyn*

# Market town

In 1355 Edward the Black Prince gave Pwllheli its charter as a borough. This brought certain privileges to the residents and granted permission for two annual fairs and a weekly Sunday market to be held. Fairs had actually been held in the town for centuries before this. For these favours Pwllheli had to pay the Crown an annual tax of £14.

In towns such as Caernarfon and Conwy, Edward I had expelled the rebellious Welsh inhabitants from inside the town walls and replaced them with his own loyal countrymen. But this never happened in Pwllheli or in Nefyn, granted its charter at the same time. Both towns in Llŷn remained essentially Welsh.

The early years of the 15th century were tempestuous ones in Wales. In September 1400 the rebel hero Owain Glyndŵr was declared *Tywysog Cymru* (Prince of Wales), and towns that had received recognition from the King of England became a target for the insurgents. Cricieth was razed and its castle destroyed. And there was no pardon for Pwllheli, however Welsh its residents, for receiving favours from the English Crown. The town was attacked and left almost deserted with its population forced to flee.

Glyndŵr's dream of political and religious independence struck a chord with a high proportion of the people of Wales. Historians see this as the most united period in Welsh history. But Owain's influence waned as the Crown tightened its grip, and by the end of the decade the uprising was virtually over. Owain died around 1415. His burial place was never disclosed and poets and romantics dreamt that he would rise again to lead his people to freedom. But in Pwllheli as elsewhere, poverty and anarchy were the immediate outcome of the rebellion, and order was not restored until the end of the century.

Pwllheli gradually outgrew Nefyn and became the main trading centre for Llŷn and parts of Eifionydd and Arfon. Until the mid-20th century two fairs were held annually in the town, when hordes of country people would descend on the town. They were not all there for pleasure.

*1. and 2. The market hall;*
*3. The market on Y Maes*

Young men and women looking for employment would line up for scrutiny by local farmers, in a ritual reminiscent of a slave market. Many would go through the same procedure again within six months.

The funfair, once a vital part of the annual fairs, still flourishes during the summer months in its traditional location on Y Maes. The weekly open air market can be traced back to the town's charter in 1355, and is held every Wednesday throughout the year and on Wednesdays and Sundays in summer.

Part of present day Pwllheli is situated on land reclaimed from the sea. Nature began the process, with estuaries silting, rivers changing course and sand-dunes expanding between Pwllheli and Llanbedrog. Then humans lent a hand by building Cob y Dref (*Town Embankment*) and Cob Glandon in 1813-14, to provide a haven for ships. At the beginning of the 20th century the harbour was developed and sluice gates installed. The way that the geography of the town has changed is indicated by some of its street names. Y Traeth (*beach*) and Lôn Dywod (*tywod:*

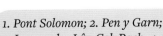
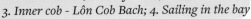
1. *Pont Solomon;* 2. *Pen y Garn;*
3. *Inner cob - Lôn Cob Bach;* 4. *Sailing in the bay*

WEST END PARADE, PWLLHELI

sand) are now some distance from the sea that used to reach what is now the town centre. In recent times global warming has caused some concern that the sea might strike back and reclaim its territory.

In 1823 a Cardiff entrepreneur and businessman called Solomon Andrews paid a visit to Pwllheli when on holiday in Llandudno. Taking a walk from the old railway station into town he was stunned by the scenery and business potential. That visit has left its mark on the town to this day. Andrews bought land by the seaside where he developed the prom, rows of houses, bandstands, the recreation ground and golf course, and a tramline where horse-drawn carriages would carry people along the shore to Llanbedrog. The tramline came to grief in a storm but most of Andrews' other developments still stand, and his name survives in Ffordd Caerdydd/*Cardiff Road* and Pont Solomon.

The close links between the town and surrounding countryside was until recently reflected in the names of the town's shops. Well-off farmers would bequeath their farms to their eldest sons and buy shops in town for younger siblings. These shops would then adopt the name of the family farm. Hirwaun House and Siop Caerhydderch were two examples and Pwlldefaid, named after a farm in Uwchmynydd is still open as a craft shop and gallery.

*1. South Beach, Pwllheli;*
*2. An old postcard of South Beach*

# Great houses

'*Pobol fawr*' translates as 'big people', but in Llŷn the term has an alternative meaning. It describes the gentry, people who are, or think they are, a step above the common people. Their houses are often referred to as Plas (palace), although they may not necessarily be bigger than a decently sized farmhouse. The peninsula is dotted with these mansions which are a fascinating part of the area's story.

**Pennarth Fawr** is a 15th century mansion between Llanarmon and the Pwllheli to Cricieth main road. The stone house includes a medieval hall with a carved truss rising from floor to ceiling. Scientific Recent scientific tests have dated this to around 1460.

A recent owner, Keith E.Houghton, researched its history thoroughly and published a book, Pennarth Fawr: a History of a Medieval Hall-house. He concludes that a much older house once occupied the site.

The original family of Pennarth Fawr can be traced back to Collwyn ap Tangno, the chief landowner in Eifionydd in the 11th century. His name survives in Cefn Collwyn, a farm near Cricieth. The most famous member of the family was Hywel ap Gruffudd or *Hywel y Fwyall* ('Hywel of the axe') who led a Welsh contingent to battle at Crécy in France in 1346 under the banner of the same Black Prince who gave Pwllheli its charter.

Collwyn owned several houses in Eifionydd but Pennarth Fawr is the only one still standing. Above a fireplace in the hall is the Coat of Arms of Collwyn ap Tangno, carved in stone. It displays a shield with three fleurs-de-lis. The Coat of Arms is described in a poem by 14th century poet Gruffydd Gryg. Gruffydd was a prominent member of *Beirdd yr Uchelwyr* (Poets of the Gentry), who played a prominent part in the social and cultural life of Wales. Until that event they had been sponsored by the Welsh Princes to entertain them and sing their praises. After the fall of Llywelyn the responsibility for their keep was transferred to the Welsh landowners. The wealthiest gentry employed the best poets, who enjoyed the

*Architectural heritage at Pennarth Fawr*

same luxuries as their sponsors. But they had to work hard for their keep. Composing the poems was not enough: they were often asked to sing them as well, to their own harp accompaniment.

**Castellmarch** near Abersoch is the location of one of Wales' best-known legends. It's now a farmhouse, but according to tradition it was once the site of a castle occupied by March Amheirchion, one of King Arthur's knights. March had a secret which he was determined to conceal from the world: he was born with a horse's ears. So he kept his hair long, and on the rare occasion when he had a haircut the servant assigned the task would thereafter disappear for ever. But the secret came out when a musician who had been summoned to play at a banquet in the castle went to a nearby bog to gather reeds for his flute. What the guests heard, instead of music, was a loud whisper declaring that March had a horse's ears. One of the murdered ex-barbers had been buried among the reeds.

A more recent story concerns Sir William Jones, squire of Castellmarch in the 17th century. Sir William was fed up with his butler, but there was no way of getting rid of him. Whenever Sir William tried to dismiss him the disloyal servant would only laugh.

But Sir Williams had connections with local smugglers. He paid them money to snatch the butler, take him away on a ship and dump him on some shore so far away that he would never again set foot in Castellmarch.

But the plot went wrong. During his time on the ship the butler befriended the crew and made such an impression that they eventually made him captain. He used his new influence to exact revenge. So the smugglers once again visited Castellmarch, this time to snatch Sir William and introduce him to distant places. After his involuntary exile he was eventually freed and allowed to return to Castellmarch a chastened man.

**Plas Glyn-y-Weddw** in Llanbedrog was built in 1856 by Lady Elizabeth Love Jones Parry of Madryn, another mansion at the foot of Garn Fadryn. Her husband had just

*1. Castellmarch – today's farm;*
*2. Reeds on the banks of Afon Soch*

died, and she was the widow who gave her name to her new acquisition (Glyn: glen; gweddw: widow). A coach would transport her there every week from Madryn, although it's said that she never spent a night at her new acquisition.

Her son, Sir Thomas Duncombe Love Jones-Parry, was the most famous member of her family. He was one of the founders of the Welsh settlement in Patagonia which is why an Argentinian city is still called Puerto Madryn, now officially twinned with Nefyn Community Council because of the Jones-Parry connection.

In 1894 Plas Glyn-y-Weddw was sold to Solomon Andrews who established the western terminal of his tramline from Pwllheli near its entrance. He opened an art gallery and tearoom there, along with a dancehall where visitors could enjoy themselves before catching the horse-drawn tram back to Pwllheli.

The Plas was sold in 1946 and declined rapidly until 1990 when it was bought by local artist Gwyneth ap Tomos and her husband Dafydd. They renovated the building and reopened it as an art gallery once more. It is now looked after by a trust, has an attractive restaurant in the old conservatory and attracts 20,000 visitors a year. An impressive amphitheatre was recently opened in the grounds, with support from descendants of Solomon Andrews.

*Plas Glyn-y-Weddw and a few of its features*

# Porth Dinllaen, shipwrecks and golf

The bustle of **Porth Dinllaen** in its prime as a port and shipbuilding centre has been vividly captured in the lyrics of John Glyn Davies. Born in Liverpool in 1980 and brought up in a Welsh-speaking household in the city, he used to spend his summer holidays in his grandfather's house in Edern. He got to know some of the old sailors of the area, and their stories and sea shanties inspired his lyrics to some of the best-known songs in the Welsh language.

Many of these feature *'Fflat Huw Puw'*, the popular name for a ship officially called the Ann Pugh. In the best-known of the songs a young boy watches the ship sailing out of Porth Dinllaen and dreams of being old enough to be a 'real sailor' on board wearing a shiny-peaked cap and with silver buttons on his coat. The real-life story of the Ann Pugh was less romantic. Having survived many perils on the high seas, it finally came to grief in a storm off the southern coast of Llŷn in 1885.

Several ships were wrecked while seeking shelter at The Roads, between Abersoch and Ynysoedd Sant Tudwal. The cause of their doom was usually Sarn Badrig, the reef associated with the legend of Cantre'r Gwaelod. The treacherous sea at Porth Neigwl fully justified the English name of the bay – *Hell's Mouth*. The worst tragedy happened at the end of the 19th century when 16 small ships from Porthmadog were trapped in the bay during a vicious storm that wrecked them all except one.

When an Italian ship carrying potatoes was wrecked in the Roads, the crew were given accommodation in Talafon, a well-known family shop in Abersoch. They showed their gratitude by leaving some of their cargo behind, and 'tatws bach Talafon' yielded crops that fed local families for years afterwards.

Across the peninsula, Porth Dinllaen provided a safe haven for many ships and sailors. In 1804 a total of 700 ships sought refuge there, including 100 during one stormy month. Just before the lifeboat station opened in 1864, 13 ships went aground within one day.

*1. Porth Dinllaen; 2. The new lifeboat station; 3. Part of the golf course*

At **Porth Tŷ Mawr**, Llangwnnadl, the rusted skeleton of an iron sailing ship can be seen at low tide. No lives were lost when the *Stuart* was wrecked on Easter Sunday 1901. It was the nature of the cargo that turned the Stuart into a legend. It was Wales's version of *Whisky Galore*, and the cove where it landed was re-christened 'Porth Wisgi'.

It was on its way from Liverpool to Newfoundland when it came to grief. The official enquiry decided that it had not been sailed in 'proper and seamanlike manner'. The locals' verdict, with no evidence, was that the captain and crew had been drinking the cargo. So everyone joined in the fun, despite the best efforts of Customs officers to stop the looting, and prophesies of doom by the temperance movement. A few whisky bottles off the *Stuart* still survive, unopened, in local homes.

Looting from shipwrecks was a respectable and accepted practice that helped to make ends meet. Locals had a bonanza when a ship called the *Lefesig* went aground not far from Porth Tŷ Mawr.

The reward this time was wheat and barley, meat and butter, and the cove became known as Porth Fesyg.

It was from Porth Fesyg that three brothers from Rhoshirwaun went out in a boat in June 1933 to set lobster pots, defying the stormy conditions. Their bodies were discovered over the next few days, and one of Wales' best poets R. Williams Parry composed a verse which is inscribed on their gravestone.

Porth Dinllaen today is very different place from its heyday as a port and shipbuilding centre, but its idyllic location ensures that it's still a lively place in summer. The lifeboat is still busy, especially in the tourist season. A new £2.7m craft, the John D Spicer, was launched in 2012, named after its Oxfordshire-based benefactor. The village is owned by the National Trust. Vehicles are only allowed through a permit, and most visitors get there by walking along the beach from Morfa Nefyn or along a path through Clwb Golff Nefyn. The golf course is regarded as possibly the most scenic in the UK, and made a favourable impression on visitors when the Ryder Cup came to Wales in 2010.

*1. and 2.Debris from the Stuart on the rocks;*
*3. Porth Tŷ Mawr*

Perhaps the biggest draw to the village now is the 170-year-old Tŷ Coch pub. In 2013 it was voted the third best beach bar in the world.

# The train now arriving…

Pwllheli station, opened in 1909, must be one of the most durable 'temporary' buildings in Wales. The wooden structure was meant to be replaced soon after by a more permanent one. But the building is still standing, and looking smarter than ever after a recent facelift. More importantly, trains still use the station, which is the northern terminal of the Cambrian Coast Railway. This line escaped the Doctor Beeching axe in the 1960s, and subsequent plans to close were shelved after fierce opposition.

There are few more scenic train journeys than the one from Pwllheli to Abermaw/Barmouth, Aberdyfi and Machynlleth, with the sea on one side and the mountains on the other. At Machynlleth passengers can change trains to Aberystwyth, or continue inland to Welshpool, Shrewsbury and Birmingham. The line between Pwllheli and Machynlleth did close for 18 months in 2014-15 when faults were detected in the 150-year-old Pont Briwet viaduct between Penrhyndeudraeth and Harlech. Travellers had to endure a much longer journey by road until the line was re-opened.

The story of the railway in Pwllheli goes back to the mid-19th century. Local people had been waiting patiently to be connected by train to the outside world when their hopes were boosted by two companies simultaneously. In 1850 the Aberystwyth and Welsh Coast Railway Company was formed to establish a service from *Pwllheli to Aberystwyth, and the Caernarvonshire Railway Company* to run one through the heart of Eifionydd from Pwllheli to Caernarfon.

Pwllheli's first train engine, called the *Castell Deudraeth*, arrived in town's harbour on a ship in 1865. Trucks were hooked to it and loads of excited residents were carried along the newly laid track to nearby Abererch two years before the line was officially open. There were other trips on the line before the official opening, including an ill-fated one on the Eifionydd line. The train from Caernarfon was packed with children and adults on their way home from a Methodist 'Sasiwn' in Caernarfon when it

*The station house at Pwllheli*

was derailed at Bryncir and six people were killed.

Pwllheli's first station was at Glandon half a mile from the town centre. A signal box from the early days still stands near a railway crossing, and is now a private house. The old station building can also be seen, but not at Pwllheli. It was demolished in 1910 and re-erected at Aberdyfi, and later moved to Llanuwchllyn near Y Bala, where it still serves the Llyn Tegid Narrow Gauge Railway. When the harbour was developed in Pwllheli at the beginning of the 20th century the line was extended to the town centre over land reclaimed from the sea.

The original intention had been to locate the northern terminus of the line not at Pwllheli but five miles further north at Porth Dinllaen. For a long time Porth Dinllaen had been in contention for development as the main port linking London and Dublin. When Parliament decided narrowly that Holyhead would be the choice, the idea of extending the railway beyond Pwllheli was abandoned.

Although the line from Pwllheli to Machynlleth was spared the Beeching axe, the line through Eifionydd to Caernarfon was not so lucky. It closed in the 1960s and much of the old route is now a cycle track. Perhaps the best known of the disused station is at Afon-wen, immortalised by popular singer Bryn Fôn in his song 'Ar y trên i Afon-wen'.

*1. An old Pwllheli tram;*
*2.Today's train at the platform*

# The village that grew

Abersoch, with its 1000 residents, is the biggest village in Llŷn. And that's in the winter, before holidaymakers arrive in droves to swell the population. With its southern aspect, relatively warm climate, palm trees, golden beaches and luxury apartments, there's a Mediterranean feel about it that sets it slightly apart from the rest of the peninsula. Its indigenous residents are in a minority in summer, but would frown at any suggestion that their village is anything other than Welsh.

Fishing and boat building were the traditional sources of employment. 'At Abersoch, consisting of a few houses upon the edge of the St Tudwal's Road, vessels are occasionally built...' That was how the traveller Edmund Hyde-Hall described the scene around 1800. Between the middle of the 18th and the middle of the 19th centuries, 14 small ships were built in the harbour. It was the 1880s, after the railway had arrived in Pwllheli, that saw the beginning of the transformation of Abersoch into a tourist haven.

By the 1950s 'keeping visitors' had become a way of life for many local families. Moving the family to a shed or caravan for a couple of months in order to let the house to strangers was not an ideal lifestyle, but it brought some welcome extra cash towards bringing up the children when good jobs were in short supply. At the start of every year the business of 'letting' would become a main topic of conversation among the women, a couple of 'empty' weeks in July a matter for concern. When summer arrived the locals would watch out for the return of familiar faces, as they would for migrating birds.

During the 1970s the change in the character of Abersoch accelerated sharply. Slack planning regulations led to large private housing estates out of proportion to local needs. In parts of the village nearly all the houses are in darkness throughout the winter months.

There are still a few lobster fishermen in the area, but tourism is by far the biggest employer. The tourist boom has given the village a prosperous look, with a good variety of shops, bars and restaurants. There is a lively social scene in summer, with a jazz festival, golf

*Abersoch harbour*

tournaments, wakeboarding and a week-long regatta. The flip side is that house prices are way out of reach of most local people in an area where wages are well below average. A four-bedroom house was recently advertised at £3.5m, building plots at £850,000 and a tiny beach hut was sold in 2015 for £100,000. When the contentious issue of second homes crops up in Wales, Abersoch is often cited as an example of what to avoid.

Many people who began to visit the area as tourists liked what they saw and became permanent residents. Some of these made notable contributions to the life of the community, none more so than a leading barrister, Sir William Howard Winterbotham and his wife Elizabeth. Having moved to live in a house they had built, Craig y Môr, they funded the building of the village hall in memory of their son Harold, who died of TB in 1913. Their generosity is noted in a plaque above entrance of the hall, built a year later.

At around the same period smallholders in nearby Cilan, led by Laura Jones, were in dispute with Francis Cooper Dunville Smythe, who had bought a cottage and some land in the area.

Smythe tried to fence off part of Mynydd Cilan, common land with a long tradition of grazing rights. Sir William Winterbotham represented the farmers in a High Court appeal and won their case.

The village hall is still a busy cultural and social centre in the village. Every summer it houses an extensive exhibition of local photographs and memorabilia, organised by volunteers.

The lifeboat played an important part in the life of the community since 1869. Generations of children would flock to watch their heroes having their weekly practice, and today the lifeboat's open day is one of the highlights of the summer. The new £214,000 craft, the Peter and Ann Setten, has been funded by a bequest from Mrs Constance Ann Setten. The nature of the calls reflects the changes in sea traffic and in the character of Abersoch. For several decades the vast majority of calls involved ships in trouble in the Roads and adjoining areas. Nowadays speedboats, jetskis and swimmers account for most emergencies.

The latest inspection report on Abersoch primary school noted that only

*Sea and beach sport at Abersoch*

90    *Exploring Pwllheli and Llŷn*

25% of the children came from homes where Welsh was the everyday language, an increase from the 5% six years previously. Some of the ex-pupils from English-speaking homes have excelled in Welsh language literary competitions. Some of their parents are also learning the language of their adopted home.

1. Abersoch inner harbour; 2.The village;
3. The bay from Bwlch Tocyn;
4. Tywyn y Fach and Mynydd Tirycwmwd

# Guardians of culture

The threat by the old Caernarfonshire County Council to close the village school at Llanaelhaearn in the early 1970s set off a train of events whose effects are still felt in the area. An action committee was set up to save the school, and having won that fight they went on to form a cooperative, Antur Aelhaearn, to create jobs that would stem the flow of young people from the village. The Antur is still going although it suffered a setback when its application to erect a wind turbine in the area was rejected after a debate that split the community.

The driving force in struggle to save the school and in forming Antur Aelhaearn was Dr Carl Clowes, a young GP in the village at that time. He was also behind an even more ambitious scheme to transform the abandoned quarrying village of Nant Gwrtheyrn into a centre for learning Welsh. Even his supporters had strong doubts – the steep and twisting road to the village was virtually impassable, and the village houses had declined almost beyond repair. But Dr Clowes persuaded people that his plan was feasible and a trust was set up to move things forward. The quarry company agreed to sell the village to the Trust for £25,000, the money was raised from various sources, the road improved and the houses renovated one by one.

The National Welsh Language and Heritage Centre at Nant Gwrtheyrn holds residential courses for learners throughout the year and is also a popular venue for weddings, conferences and curious visitors drawn to a truly enchanted place between the mountains and the sea. The café, Caffi Meinir, is named after the legend of young lovers Rhys and Meinir. There was a tradition that the bride would go and hide on the morning of her wedding. Rhys and the guests assembled in the church in Clynnog on the big day but there was no sign of Meinir. Rhys's friends went to look for her, in vain. After months of heartbreak Rhys became resigned to her disappearance and not knowing her fate. then one night during a fierce thunderstorm he went to shelter under an oak tree in Nant Gwrtheyrn when lightning split the tree in half. There

*Nant Gwrtheyrn, following recent alterations*

in the hollow trunk he saw the skeleton of his bride in her wedding dress. He died of a heart attack, and the spirits of the young lovers are said to walk the beach of Nant Gwrtheyrn.

* * *

A plaque on a pet supplies shop in Pwllheli commemorates another initiative by people intent on preserving Wales' language and identity. Only six men attended a meeting held in what was then a temperance hotel during the National Eisteddfod in the town in August 1925. The meeting was not reported in any newspaper, but it was there that Plaid Cymru, the National Party of Wales, was formed. Not one of the founders was a conventional politician. They were people of diverse backgrounds united by their patriotism. Moses Griffith was an agricultural economist; H.R.Jones a grocery salesman; Saunders Lewis, a lecturer; Fred Jones and Lewis Valentine were both ministersof religion; and David Edmund Williams was a carpenter.

In 1936 Saunders Lewis and Lewis Valentine along with writer and teacher D.J.Williams were back in Pwllheli. In the early hours of September 8, they went to the police station and told a stunned constable that they had set fire to buildings at an RAF training station in nearby Penyberth. The decision to locate the 'bombing school' in Llŷn had incensed many people, after possible sites in England were rejected on grounds of social and environmental disruption. The issue became a national cause celebre. When constitutional methods had failed, the three unlikely arsonists resorted to direct action. The jury at Caernarfon failed to agree, so their case was transferred to the Old Bailey where they were found guilty and sentenced to nine months in Wormwood Scrubs. A plaque near a caravan park and golf course in Penrose pays homage to the three unlikely arsonists.

* * *

A plaque on a shop in Stryd Penlan marks the birthplace of Pwllheli's most famous son. Sir Albert Evans-Jones, better known

by his bardic name Cynan, was a popular and lyrical poet, an ordained minister with a majestic voice, a dramatist, lecturer and fisherman. A stalwart of the National Eisteddfod for much of the 20th century, as Arch druid he brought some of his love of order and formality to the festival's main ceremonies. He was also an independent spirit. To commemorate his becoming a Freeman of Pwllheli, the Town Council commissioned a local artist to paint an oil portrait of him. The painting still hangs in the council chamber. Cynan rejected it because he thought it made him look old. More recently, a bronze bust of Cynan was sculptered by John Meirion Morris and is on display at Pwllheli library.

Born in 1895, he served in the Great War as a soldier and chaplain. In 1921 he won the Crown at the National Eisteddfod for a poem, Mab y Bwthyn (*The Cottage Boy*) based on his war experiences in Macedonia. In the poem, he reminisces about fetching water for his grandmother from Ffynnon Felin Bach, a well on the outskirts of Pwllheli. There is now a plaque on the well, with a quotation from the poem.

*1. Stryd Penlan; 2. Cynan on a pub sign; 3. Ffynnon Felin Bach; 4. Cynan's portrait?*

# On the beach

'I don't know what it is about these little beaches that excites me so much when I come down to them. I never feel anything like that about the ones on the southern side. I have been to Aberdaron beach many times, to Porth Cadfan with my father, to Porth Ysgo and to Ynysgain Fawr and Tynymorfa, but not one of these has that thing that you have no idea how to describe – that you get in Porth Tŷ Mawr, and indeed to some extent in every cove from Porth Ysgaden to Porthor.'

The above is a rough translation of a passage from *Pigau'r Sêr*, a lyrical account of his childhood by the writer J.G.Williams. He was describing a visit with his grandmother to Porth Tŷ Mawr, where the whisky ship *Stuart* went aground. Beaches on the southern coast of the peninsula also have their advantages – they tend to be more accessible and marginally warmer for a start. But many people will identify with the sense of undefinable magic in some of the coves between Llangwnnadl and Aberdaron.

The best known of these is Porthor, a sandy beach owned by the National Trust who also provide a car park and toilets. Porthor's main claim to fame is the fine texture of the sand which makes a whistling sound when people walk on it; hence the unofficial but well-known name *Whistling Sands*. A previous owner tried to cash in on this by offering small samples of the sand for sale in polythene bags. It made tabloid headlines and caused a bit of mirth, but there were not many customers. There is now a shop and café on the beach, but they don't sell sand.

Perhaps the most accessible beach of all is Aberdaron, within yards of the centre of the village. There is a spectacular view from the patio of the Tŷ Newydd Hotel overlooking the fine sandy beach towards Ynysoedd Gwylan (*Gwylan*: seagull), sometimes mistaken by newcomers for Ynys Enlli. A well-known Welsh poem states that Enlli cannot be seen from the sea shore.

Porth Iago is a delightful little beach near Porthor, approached through a farmyard and down a steep footpath, but is extremely popular despite its remoteness. Heading east towards Nefyn

*Aberdaron beach*

1. Porthor; 2. Porth Iago;
3. Porth Ceiriad; 4. Pentraeth

you encounter several small, pebbly coves until you get to Llangwnnadl and Traeth Penllech with its long stretch of sand. Tudweiliog, Porth Dinllaen, Morfa Nefyn and Nefyn all have pretty and accessible beaches. There has been some coastal erosion on this section. In Nefyn in 2001 a landslide swept two cars off a clifftop path killing one of the occupants.

Beaches on the northern coastline tend to be more open and less craggy than those in the south. Porth Neigwl and Porth Ceiriad with their spectacular waves are popular with surfers. In the Abersoch area there is a long bow of fine sandy beaches between Trwyn Cilan and Llanbedrog, bearing resonant names such as Traeth Marchros, Traeth Lleferin, Traeth Tywyn y Fach, Traeth Castellmarch and Glan Môr Gwaith. *'Gwaith'* (works) refers to old quarrying activity on Mynydd Tir Cwmwd. Ar low tide you can walk most of the way from Llanbedrog to Pwllheli along the beach, and onward to Abererch, Penychain and Cricieth with only occasional diversions inland. In Llŷn you are never far away from a beautiful beach, and the Llŷn section of the Wales Coastal Path will guide you on your way.

*1. Glan Môr Gwaith; 2. Llanbedrog;*
*3. Porth Neigwl*

# Sailing to glory

The transition from boat-building and fishing to sailing of pleasure as a sport started early in Abersoch, with the annual regatta going back to 1880s. Aberdaron also has a long history of sailing races, now organised by Cymdeithas Hwylio Hogia Llŷn, a group of local enthusiasts. They use the traditional clinker-built boats of Llŷn. There are no classes and every boat is different. Points are awarded for every race and whoever heads the table at the end of the season is crowned champion of Aberdaron bay.

The most exciting marine development in recent times is Plas Heli, home of the Welsh National Sailing Academy and Events Centre. Pwllheli Sailing Club was established in 1958 and Plas Heli is its fifth and most impressive home. Unlike Abersoch, where the Sailing Club is run mainly by people from outside the area, Pwllheli has retained a strong degree of local control and the Welsh language has a prominent role in its activities. The town has produced a number of distinguished yachtsmen, none more so than Richard Tudor, who three times skippered boats in the world's toughest yacht race, the round-the-world challenge going westward, regarded by sailors as the wrong way. Richard is now in charge of vocational courses in seamanship at the local Sixth Form college, Coleg Meirion Dwyfor.

Pwllheli with its superb sailing waters, spectacular scenery and 400-berth marina is recognised as one of the best yachting venues in Europe. Various schemes have been put forward over the years to expand and develop the facilities, provoking fierce arguments at times between supporters intent on generating business and opponents concerned about the environmental and cultural impact. One scheme would have put more emphasis on speedboats than sailing yachts, which its supporters said would create more jobs, whereas opponents spoke of noise and pollution. There were plans to incorporate a hotel development, which most people would approve of, and chalet accommodation that many feared would change the linguistic balance of the town.

*The new sailing centre, Plas Heli, at Pwllheli*

In the end there was a consensus in favour of the £9m Plas Heli centre, funded by the Welsh Government, the European Union and Gwynedd Council.

A key aim of the Sailing Academy is to train local youngsters to take advantage of their maritime heritage. During its first summer of operation in 2015 Plas Heli hosted five major events, attracting competitors from scores of countries world-wide. This generated millions of pounds of income to the town and an estimated 35.000 'bed nights' in accommodation in the town and adjoining areas.

Plas Heli is an impressive building that is permanently illuminated by an energy efficient LED system, with the lights changing colour in reaction to wind strength and direction. Plas Heli has a restaurant and bar, and facilities for concerts and meetings. The local community is encouraged to make full use of the centre, which also works in partnership with the marine engineering and boat building course run by Richard Tudor at Coleg Meirion Dwyfor.

*Some of the anchorages at Pwllheli*

The venue had an unexpected boost early in 2016 when Plas Heli came joint first in an online poll of sailing bars around the world. Plas Heli is a key partner in the Ecoamgueddfa project described in the next chapter.

The days of Pwllheli as a major fishing and shipbuilding centre are long gone, but the sea still plays a major part in the economic, social and cultural life of the town.

# The Ecomuseum

We now return to the Ecoamgueddfa (*amgueddfa*: museum) development mentioned in the opening chapter. The Ecomuseum movement originated in France in the early 1970s and has since spread to many countries worldwide. Ecoamgueddfa, located in Llŷn, is the first to be set up in Wales. Its website (http://www.ecoamgueddfa.org/) defines the concept as follows:

An ecomuseum celebrates the identity of a place and is largely based on local participation, aiming to enhance the welfare and development of local communities. The term 'eco' specifically refers to ecology rather than economic. There is no particular model for an ecomusuem but the one common element is that they all share the same vision...

The Ecoamgueddfa's vision is to see an increase in cultural tourism, leading to a year round sustainable tourist industry, that will bring economic benefits to the area as well as social. The Ecoamgueddfa will operate by using digital media in a innovative and positive way to increase community evolvement, and attract a world-wide audience to this unique and beautiful area.

Describing itself as a 'museum without walls', the Ecoamgueddfa operates in partnership with seven of Llŷn's heritage organisations: Nant Gwrtheyrn, Llŷn Maritime Museum, Felin Uchaf, Porth y Swnt, Plas yn Rhiw, Oriel Plas Glyn-y-Weddw. Three of these have been described in previous chapters. We'll now take a brief look at the other four.

## Llŷn Maritime Museum

Of all the participating organisations in the Ecoamgueddfa, this is possibly the one that most resembles a conventional museum, and the only one with Amgueddfa/Museum in its title. Located in the disused church in the centre of town, the weather vane on its roof is a clear indication of the area's maritime past. The

*The church which houses the Maritime Museum at Nefyn*

first church was built on the site in the 6th century and the present building dates from 1827. It ceased being used as a parish church when a new one was built in 1901.

The existence of the Museum is testimony to concerted effort over many years by the whole community. A group of volunteers set up the first museum in 1977 to display itms of interest. But the building was in a bad state and the museum had to close in 2000 because of health and safety concerns.

In 2007, the community set up a new committee to reopen the museum, and a package of funding was secured from various sources. It now has a permanent exhibition, a café, shop and small stage. It holds a collection of around 400 artefacts associated with the maritime heritage of Nefyn and the Llŷn Peninsula.

## Felin Uchaf

It would take more space than is available here to do justice to the range and uniqueness of the activities of Menter y Felin Uchaf (menter: enterprise; melin: mill; uchaf: upper). Like the language learning centre at Nant Gwrtheyrn, it was born mainly through the vision and determination of one man. Dafydd Davies-Hughes brought together a group of friends to raise funds to buy Felin Uchaf farm at Rhoshirwaun in 2004. Their vision, according to their website http://www.felinuchaf.org/ was

> to create a place where people and the land on which they worked could nourish each other in body, soul and spirit and to found a Community Enterprise Centre based on a holistic approach to environmental and cultural education.

They have since, again in their own words transformed the landscape through planting thousands of trees, reinstating hedgerows and wetland habitats and sculpting new eco buildings out of stone, earth, thatch and timber harvested locally. On what used to be a bare, windswept site there are now a patchwork of small gardens and flowered meadows, a low green haze of young trees and the fruits of many people's labours: paths that lead to secluded roundhouses, to a

*1. The Maritime Museum; 2. Inside; 3. The shipwrecked Stewart at the museum*

subterranean hall where stories and songs and the arts are celebrated, to workspaces for the sharing of fine craftsmanship and a community garden for people to cooperatively grow herbs and vegetables in a sustainable, life enhancing way.

The centre runs courses and workshops in rural crafts, hosts cultural events and sells its own produce through a farm shop. Much of the work is done by volunteers. The centre is open all year round and well worth a visit.

**Porth y Swnt**

Situated in the car park in Aberdaron, the furthest village on the peninsula, Porth y Swnt is a recent facility built and owned

*Various craft buildings at Felin Uchaf*

by the National Trust. Defined as an interpretive centre rather than a museum, it does not tell the story of the area in a simple, direct way. Using poetry, sculpture and other subtle devices it seeks to create an atmosphere, stimulate curiosity and the urge to delve further into the history, culture and natural environment of the area. Some will leave inspired, and even those without the patience to enter the mood will appreciate a pleasant place to shelter on a rainy day.

## Plas yn Rhiw

This other National Trust property a couple of miles from Aberdaron could hardly be more different from Porth y Swnt. Located in woodland on the slope of Mynydd Rhiw overlooking Porth Neigwl, the present house is a modestly sized manor dating from the early 17th century. It's said athat the original house on the site was built by local chieftain Meirion Goch in the 10th century. But the area was occupied centuries earlier. There is evidence of prehistoric activity in the area,

including neolithic burial chambers and the axe factory already mentioned.

Plas yn Rhiw was deserted in 1922 and left to deteriorate until it was bought in 1939 by three sisters, Eileen, Lorna and Honora Keating, who had traced their ancestry to the original owners of the manor. They restored the house and garden to their former glory.

1. *Inside the main circular hut, Felin Uchaf;*
2. *Snowdrops at Plas yn Rhiw*

# 'Yma o hyd'

So is the glass half full or half empty? If you ask a sample of the residents how they see the future of Llŷn, opinions will vary widely between hope and despair. Some will have noticed every empty shop and boarded-up pub in Pwllheli, closed rural schools, doctor shortages, ageing congregations in the few remaining chapels, the drift of young people to Cardiff or over the border, and the increasing use of English in areas that used to be strongholds of Welsh. Others will see the opening of new shops, restaurants and art galleries, small rural businesses emerging, some exiles returning home and an increasing number of incomers identifying with the language and culture of their adopted land.

There is plenty of evidence to support the half full and half empty perceptions. Comparatively remote areas like Llŷn are particularly vulnerable to Government cutbacks that put pressure on local councils and public services. At the time of writing, a campaign has been launched to ensure that Neuadd Dwyfor, a cinema, concert venue, library and tourist information centre in Pwllheli, does not come under the axe. Hardly a week goes by without local newspapers voicing concerns about threats to close a public toilet or cottage hospital, raise domestic and business rates or reduce the frequency of litter collections. But pressure can stimulate a community's determination to buck the trend and create jobs. They are aided by the digital revolution that makes geographic remoteness less of a handicap than in the past. And increased awareness of global warming and environmental issues has put added value on using local produce. Craft and art and local material are featured in art galleries in Pwllheli. We return now to some of the recent communal initiatives mentioned in our opening chapter.

**Glasu** is an ice cream produced by a family in Edern, following traditional recipes and using milk from their own dairy herd. The quality of the pasture at the farm, Bryn Rhydd, was recognised recently when it won the National Grassland Management award.

*1. & 2. A gallery in Pwllheli; 3. Tafarn y Fic, Llithfaen – the oldest village pub cooperative in Europe*

**Becws Islyn**, situated on one of three steep hills leading down to Aberdaron, is a new building on the site of a much older bakery. Being the only building in the village with a thatched roof, and considerably higher than the corrugated iron hut it replaced, it can hardly be missed by visitors. It sells a variety of fresh bread, cakes, pies and sausage rolls, and the tearoom upstairs has a unique

1. *Becws Islyn;*
2. *and 3. Heritage on the tearoom walls*

collection of murals featuring local history. The characters depicted include the Last King of Enlli and Dic Aberdaron, probably the area's most famous son. Richard Robert Jones was an eccentric genius, a well-travelled tramp, cat lover and linguist who, it is claimed, could speak up to 15 languages.

**Oinc Oink** is the imaginative name of a company that rears free range pigs and supplies a range of pork products from their family farm in Llithfaen. They take pride in keeping their pigs happy and healthy, and believe that this helps to provide exceptionally tender and lean pork.

**Cwrw Llŷn** is a cooperative micro-brewery set up by 12 friends who produced their first beer in May 2011. The enterprise started in an old cowshed in Llwyndyrys using third-hand equipment, with barrels being distributed to local pubs on the back of a coal lorry owned by one of the partners. Since then the operation has moved to state pf the art premises in Nefyn. The company sees itself as inheritor of the brewing tradition that goes back to the Bronze Age brewery at Porth Neigwl described in a previous chapter. The brands of beer produced today have names that reflect local or national traditions including Brenin Enlli, Seithenyn, Cochyn, Glyndwr, Y Brawd Houdini and Porth Neigwl. They are all sold in several outlets throughout the peninsula.

Cwrw Llŷn has recently won a two-year David and Goliath victory over the British Trading Standards Office and the National Measures Office in London. The company wanted to produce glasses for their brewery with their capacity indicated by the Welsh 'Peint' rather than the English 'Pint'. Because this was not a matter devolved to the Welsh Assembly the offices argued that it was exempt from the Welsh Language Act of 2011 which gave Welsh equal status with English. They also believed that the use of Peint would mislead drinkers who did not understand Welsh. The brewery responded by asking 'How many pints would a member of the

*1. The new Cwrw Llŷn brewery;*
*2. & 3. Entertainment and exhibition at the beer festival*

public need to consume before they were too tipsy to understand that they were drinking pints?' Common sense prevailed and the *Peint* received official blessing in February 2013.

In 2016 Ysgol Botwnnog, the secondary school in the heart of Llŷn celebrated its 400th anniversary. Bishop Henry Rowland who left money in his will to establish the school in 1616 stipulated that the first teacher 'a good scholar, an Oxford MA, unmarried and an Englishman'.

Four hundred years down the line, Welsh is the main teaching language in Ysgol Botwnnog and most pupils from English-speaking homes become learn the language fluently. The old belief that people cannot master more than one language is outdated, and the children of Llŷn still speak a variation of the language that was spoken in the hillforts of the area thousands of years ago. This is a story of resilience summed up in an iconic song by folk singer Dafydd Iwan – *'Ry'n ni yma o hyd'/* We are still here.

*1. Glasu; 2. OincOink; 3. A selection of local craft ale; 4. Peint!*

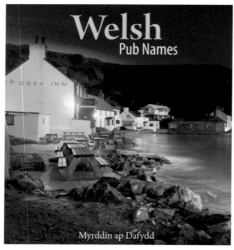

Welsh
Pub Names

Myrddin ap Dafydd

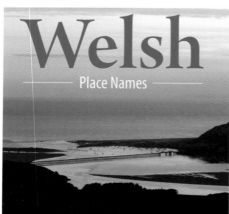

Welsh
Place Names

Welsh Poetry
in translation